Release

YOURSELF

LEGAL DISCLAIMER

---

www.instagram.com/garciainsights/
www.facebook.com/Garciainsights/
twitter.com/garciainsights
www.garciainsights.com

Book design by Olivier Darbonville

ISBN: 978-1-968537-05-0 (sc)
ISBN: 978-1-968537-06-7 (hc)
ISBN: 978-1-968537-07-4 (eBook)

Release
YOURSELF

UNLEASHING
—— YOUR ——
WARRIOR WOMAN

GARCIA HANSON

I can do all things through Christ who strengthens me.

Philippians 4:13

This verse reminds believers that they have the strength and capability to overcome challenges and achieve their goals with the help of their faith in Christ. It serves as a source of encouragement and empowerment, reminding us that we are not alone in our endeavors and that we can draw on divine strength to face any situation. This scripture is often quoted as a reminder of the power and support that comes from a strong spiritual foundation.

DEDICATION

With gratitude and hope, this book is dedicated to every woman's struggle. It is written for you who navigate a world of adversity to embrace love. On a path strewn with challenges, your unyielding spirit breaks barriers and redefines boundaries. With courage, you walk through fire and emerge tempered, strong, and resilient. Your perseverance inspires and motivates us all.

To the men who have stumbled upon these words, this dedication extends an invitation to gain insight and better your understanding. We hope you'll embrace the opportunity to grow with us. Read with an open mind and heart. Expand your perspective, dismantle preconceived notions, and listen. When support and understanding falter, your empathy and willingness to learn make a difference.

The following tapestry of women's struggles and triumphs reveals our power to create a just and inclusive world. Let this dedication serve as a call to action. From here, we will challenge the status quo and societal norms that limit possibility. Striving for equality, we will write a narrative of empathy and create a future where all may thrive, a world where love, understanding, and perseverance flourish for everyone.

Acknowledgements

As I reflect on the creation of this manuscript, I'm filled with awe and gratitude. This vision could not have come to fruition without an abundance of grace from God. In His unwavering love and guidance, I found the strength and inspiration to write these words.

To my Heavenly Father, I offer my deepest thanks. You have been my source of perseverance throughout this journey. Your wisdom has infused every page, and your divine touch has shaped every word. I am humbled by your presence, and I am eternally grateful for your unfailing love.

To my cherished family and friends, thank you for your constant support. Your encouragement, prayers, and understanding have sustained me through the challenges and joys of the writing process. You are my pillars of strength, my soundboards, and my biggest cheerleaders. Your belief in me means more than words can express.

My heartfelt appreciation goes out to the editors of this work. Your keen insights, meticulous attention to detail, and commitment to excellence have polished these pages. Your invaluable contributions have clarified the message I sought to convey.

I want to acknowledge the countless individuals whose stories and experiences have shaped this narrative. Thank you for your bravery and vulnerability. Your voices give these words power and authenticity.

And of course, I am eternally grateful to you, the reader who embarks on this journey. It is my fervent hope that the grace of God, which permeates these pages, will touch your heart and soul. May this work serve as a beacon of hope and source of encouragement, reminding you of the immense strength you possess.

I offer my profound gratitude to my loved ones, editors, readers, and all who played a role in the creation of this treasured tome. The transformative power of God's love was present in every stroke of the pen.

May His grace shine upon you all.

Opening Prayer

Dear Heavenly Father,

We humbly gather in your divine presence today to seek guidance and blessings as we embark on a journey of empowerment, healing, and growth. We come before you with hearts open and eager, ready to explore the depths of our experiences and the transformative power of our struggles.

Lord, we acknowledge your unwavering love and grace, knowing that, in our darkest moments, you are near. We find solace in your comforting embrace, and we draw strength from your divine wisdom.

As we delve into the pages of this book, may your spirit guide our words and intentions. Grant us clarity and discernment as we explore complex emotions, challenges, and triumphs. May our words uplift and inspire those who read them.

Father, we place our faith in you, knowing that you are the source of hope and restoration. We welcome you to use this book as a conduit for healing and transformation in the lives of women who feel unseen and unheard.

Let the scriptures that fill the pages of this book illuminate the path of righteousness, empowering women to embrace their God-given worth. May these words serve as a balm for wounded souls, a beacon of hope in times of despair, and a catalyst for positive change in the world.

Lord, we ask for your divine guidance and protection as we navigate the delicate terrain of healing. Strengthen us, fortify our spirits, and grant us courage, that we may face the challenges that lie ahead.

We lift up every woman who reads this book. May they find solace and a renewed sense of purpose here. Let them be reminded that they are fearfully and wonderfully made, capable of overcoming every obstacle in their path.

In your holy and precious name, we pray.

Amen

CONTENTS

PREFACE

You came into the world with bright eyes and all the confidence of a woman destined for greatness, but somewhere along the way, the ways of the world dulled your spark. Biases, selfishness, judgment, vanity, insecurity, and arrogance dripped into your bucket from the outside until the weight was too much, so you put it down and began to wait.

You waited for your partner to respect you or for the right partner to show up. You waited for the same advancement opportunities men in your field seize every day. You waited for a child, an opening to speak, a moment to be weak, a port in the storm, or just a kind word from yourself or anyone else. You waited for your path to be highlighted like the exit row of a plane, but here you sit in a jungle of options with no path in sight.

As you sit, you squeeze your eyes tight to keep out the ugliness of the world, hoping to just make it from one day to the next. You forgot how bright your fire can burn. It's time to open your eyes and light your own way with the fierce flame you hold inside.

Loving yourself wholeheartedly and setting standards and boundaries that reflect that love will change your entire life, from your relationships to your professional trajectory The coming chapters teach practical tools for real-life challenges and the importance of self-worth in a man's world.

This is your starting point, and you're not alone anymore. Beside you are thousands of women who seek a resilient, independent, conqueror's mindset. Find the clarity to dictate your future. Discover the self-worth to step away from what's holding you back. Let go of what's outside your control, forgive yourself for your mistakes and inabilities, and be inspired toward the most impactful transformation of your life.

INTRODUCTION

There is a warrior in you, a fierce and resilient spirit that embodies courage and determination. She is unapologetic, authentic, and incapable of bending to societal pressure. She embraces everything that makes her unique: her gifts, passions, dreams, flaws, and fears. She intimidates would-be predators and attracts strong, positive relationships.

As the years go by, life unfolds in twists and turns. You forget the extraordinary power you possess. Your spirit has been overshadowed, but she remains an integral part of your being. She is you. You can reawaken her and embark on a journey of self-discovery and empowerment.

This is not a journey for the faint-hearted. It requires deep introspection and the courage to step into the unknown. You'll confront fears, dismantle barriers, and embrace the full spectrum of your emotions – and the emotions of even the most buttoned-up people in your life.

From unrelenting struggle and hurtful words of discouragement to the timely identification of viable love, from translating man-speak and clawing your way up the corporate ladder to finding your voice, your femininity, your tribe, your worth, and your faith, this compilation of invaluable female insight and wisdom with guide you through some of the toughest aspect of womanhood so that you can come out undefeated on the other side.

The biggest challenge you'll face is truly believing in your worth and your power. Many of your experiences and interactions will try to deepen your worst insecurities. Toxic relationships, professional struggles, domestic pressure, and competition will beat you down with "you're not good enough" and "you can't do this" if you allow it.

You are not defined by anyone else's standards, limitations, and biases. You are not defined by your mistakes. You are a force of nature and will achieve greatness, whatever that means to you. It's never too late to remember who you are and reclaim your value.

Through this journey, you'll achieve profound growth and emotional transformation. You'll discover what it means to have your happiness come from within. In this book, you'll find tools, insights, and stories that will inspire you to connect with your inner warrior spirit. You'll learn to define success in your own terms and design a life that aligns with who you truly are, not what anyone expects you to be.

Step into each chapter with an open heart, believe in yourself, and let this collection of women's experiences, knowledge, and support guide you to where you were always meant to be.

CHAPTER 1

When Everything Falls Apart

L ife is a master of the sucker punch. One minute, you're cruising along with everything figured out, and then, when you least expect it, BAM! Suddenly, you feel like you're being tested to see how much you can take before you break.

As the ground beneath you gives way, you start to question everything. Do you deserve it? Is it karma getting justice for some obscure infraction or God Himself punishing you? Is this a random, unfortunate wave of fate, or are you a magnet for destruction?

As a woman, you wear many hats in life. You're a wife, mom, boss, colleague, sister, daughter, and everything else. There's so much going on all the time, things are bound to fall apart. The never-ending cycle of commitments and obligations leaves you feeling stretched thin.

I can't tell you how many times my life has fallen apart, and the truth is I wanted to give up every time. It's natural to want to throw in the towel in those moments. Why not wave your white flag and escape to an island paradise with an eternal spring of pina colada? But giving up is not in our DNA.

I won't sugarcoat it. Picking up the pieces and rebuilding your life is hard. It takes patience, stamina, and strength. You'll fail and fail again. Some days are so bad, you curl up in bed and cry, but every morning is a chance to try again.

Imagine a mother, overwhelmed by the demands of raising children and juggling a career. She faces sleepless nights, endless chores, and the constant battle to find time for herself, but she embraces the challenge. She nurtures her children with love and grace, and in doing so, she discovers the resilience of a warrior within herself.

Then there's the woman who was struck with heartbreak and betrayal. Her spirit is shattered, and her confidence is gone, but she finds the strength to heal. Through the tears and pain, she rebuilds herself. In her vulnerability, she discovers her true power, her inner warrior.

This journey is not easy. It requires faith – the unwavering belief that there is a purpose to every battle, every tear. As a Christian, I firmly believe in the guiding hand of God. He is the source of my strength and the anchor of my faith. As you explore the role of faith in your own life, draw upon its power to carry you through the toughest times.

Emily

Devastated by divorce, Emily chose to use her broken state as an opportunity for growth and self-discovery. Instead of allowing her circumstances to define her, she channeled that pain into her passions and achieved more than she had in 20 years of marriage.

Emily went back to school and finished her degree. With that, she got her dream job, which allowed her to buy her dream home and travel to three continents. She saw her inner strength and used it to rebuild her life. Each step forward gave her the confidence to become who she wanted to be.

Emily's story teaches us that resilience isn't about avoiding pain or failure. Resilience is simply an objective view that highlights the path ahead. By accepting the circumstances, emotions, and perceived failure, she transformed her pain into personal power. Instead of allowing a struggle to define her, she used it to gain perspective and rediscover herself.

CHAPTER 2

Sticks and Stones

W e've all heard the rhyme. "Sticks and stones may break my bones, but words will never hurt me." Baloney, right? Words have power, and we know that better than anyone. In a world where the female body is constantly targeted and criticized, we fight a constant battle to defy society's narrow definition of beauty. Our behavior is examined and criticized, weighed against a standard of behavior, and thought set by men with no consideration for the vast, essential, and wonderful differences between our two species.

From birth, we're bombarded with the world's assessment of our appearance. Well-meaning loved ones and hateful others tell you you're fat or ugly, affectionately refer to your chubby cheeks or lanky frame, and label you with "big girl" or "skin and bones." Even those given titles like "beautiful" and "heartbreaker" will feel the pressure to keep that image for their entire lives.

On top of our appearance, we're given an impossible framework for our demeanor and personality. You can't be too loud or too quiet, too smart or too simple, too assertive or too submissive. Women are always too much of something, and many of us fix it by constantly trying to be what everyone wants or giving up and accepting a role as an unappealing woman.

From the playground to social media, these judgments and expectations follow you into adulthood, being reaffirmed with every repetition. By now, your self-worth is destroyed or else completely reliant on the validation of others. You internalize every criticism, creating a breeding ground for negative self-talk.

Internal Dialogue

You are your own worst critic. You beat yourself down with "I'm not good enough" and "I can't do this." You miss opportunities because you doubt yourself or damage relationships with insecurity. You tell yourself you're not pretty enough, and when a man chooses another woman, you take that as confirmation. When you see a confident woman, you see a woman who's better than you instead of a woman who simply values herself.

The dislike you feel toward yourself wasn't created on its own, and it won't go away on its own. You won't wake up one day and feel beautiful, intelligent, and worthy unless you choose to be kind and fair to yourself. You have to say, "This stops today," and change the script. Write a new internal dialogue filled with compassion, forgiveness, and love.

Imagine waking up in the morning and looking in the mirror. Instead of telling yourself, "This is as good as it gets," or something even more hurtful, imagine saying, "Hello, beautiful. Today is going to be amazing, and you're going to achieve great things." It sounds cheesy, but changing the words you say to yourself will start your healing process and reveal a version of you that's been hidden for far too long.

External Dialogue

One traumatic experience with a man can shape all your future dating experiences. A family member can make you self-conscious for years just by saying you've gained weight. Someone having a bad day can make a hateful comment about you, and you'll believe them. No matter the intention or circumstance, the message you receive is, "You're not good enough," and it sticks.

STOP.

When you allow others to influence your self-esteem, you allow them to control your happiness – or eliminate it. People's opinions are shaped by their emotions, perspectives, histories, insecurities, cultures, and so much more. You can't control what they think or say, but you can control how you react.

An objective, mindful response to a hurtful comment might go something like this: someone says something that hurts your feelings. Instead of taking it as gospel truth, you ask yourself why this person might be saying something hurtful to you at this moment. You ask yourself if their observation might give you an opportunity to grow as a woman.

If not, the comment is unnecessary and probably not coming from a helpful place. If there is an opportunity for growth, you can ask yourself if that growth is a priority for you. Through this process, your self-esteem remains intact – in fact, you might even be proud of yourself for handling things so well – and your only responses might be to thank the person for their insight and pursue your growth opportunity if there is one.

Words can sting, but they can only break you if you let them. You have the power to determine their impact. You can let them define you, or you can use them as stepping stones toward your success. Choose to define yourself in your own words. Make your positive self-talk the loudest voice in your head.

CHAPTER 3

Love Finds You

We all want to be loved, build a stable life, and share our highs and lows with someone special. It's natural and normal to hope for that and look forward to it. It's also natural and normal to feel a little lonely sometimes when you don't have it.

Society, culture, and media exacerbate negative feelings associated with being single. They set unrealistic expectations for how and when we should find love, and they say there's something wrong with you if you haven't found it yet.

Finding love has thus become a focal point, especially for those of us in our 30s and 40s. relationships have become a source of validation both inwardly and for the world's approval. We swipe left and right, go to social settings we don't really enjoy, and overanalyze text messages like they're written in code.

Over time, it can wear you down. You compare yourself to women in seemingly happy relationships and teach yourself to expect rejection. You blame your singleness on your looks, character, or circumstances. Your self-image suffers, and you compromise your standards.

Love becomes a goal in your mind – a destination – rather than a beautiful part of life that comes along in its own time. When something does come along, you're so attracted to the idea of love, you hardly analyze what's being offered.

With little self-respect and a world of pressure, you lose your objectivity. You tell yourself it's a good thing to see the good in people, even though you know you're ignoring bad qualities that should send you running. You see financial security, a sense of humor, and a handsome face while ignoring misogyny, emotional immaturity, and disrespect.

This road leads to a relationship in which you don't feel loved, and you don't get to build and share the life you wanted. You settle for less than what you dreamed of – less than what you deserve – because it's such a relief to have someone next to you.

You can finally update your relationship status on Facebook and bring a date to the family reunion so Aunt Gertrude will get off your back. And all it cost was your dignity, happiness, and the legendary love that was meant for you.

At best, your partner is incompatible with you, and you find yourself constantly at odds. At worst, your partner is abusive.

Predators are adept at identifying potential victims – typically women with low self-worth and a strong desire to be in a relationship.

This is precisely what's wrong with the idea that a prince will rescue you. The princes of the world are not looking for women who need to be rescued. They're looking for strong, driven women who brighten the world around them by simply being their radiant selves. The men who are looking for vulnerable women are not the men you want to end up with.

Love should never hurt. It should uplift, support, and encourage you to be your best self. Your partner should love you as a whole person with all your flaws while walking side-by-side with you to improve individually and as a unit. They should respect your boundaries, listen to your dreams, and stand with you through thick and thin.

After a bad relationship – or a few bad relationships – it's common to think this idea of a good partner is a pipe dream or that it's only possible for special, perfect, beautiful women. Well, surprise. You are a special, perfect, beautiful woman, and the "perfect partner" exists for you, too.

The first thing you must realize is that love is not a destination to race towards. It's a journey you're going to take with one person for the rest of your lives. You owe it to yourself to take your time and find someone who respects you as an equal.

When you radiate self-love and confidence, you attract positive, healthy relationships. Equally importantly, you repel opportunists and insecure attachments. When you see your value, others can see it too. Then, when you meet the right person, you'll be the right person – a strong woman who is happy and whole.

Pivoting from romance to self-love isn't easy, but it's possible, and you'll feel the difference almost immediately. Instead of obsessing over love, think about what makes you happy. Go out and live your best life. Pursue your passions, surround yourself with good friends who build you up, and engage in activities that bring you joy.

Real love doesn't happen when you're looking for it. When you actively seek love, your priorities change. You present an altered version of yourself – a version that is desperate and needy – and you'll end up with someone who is compatible with that version, not the real you.

Focus on the bright, beautiful world in front of you. Be in love with yourself and your dreams. Be present in your joy, goals, and existing relationships. Love will sneak up on you as you're enjoying life and connecting with people who are compatible with the real you.

Don't watch the clock. This stage can take years, and it's worth every second. There's nothing wrong with your looks, personality, or lucky stars. It just takes time for two people who can stand the test of time to find each other. Resist the urge to compare yourself to others or engage in negative self-talk.

When someone comes along, and things seem to click, don't hang all your hopes on them prematurely. If you feel yourself diving in too fast, slow down. Discover the depth of your compatibility slowly, naturally. Get to know each other with clear, objective perspectives. Let their actions speak for them.

Sometimes, you feel compatible, and they don't. Or you know you're not compatible, but you wish things were different. This is a reality of the journey: heartbreak. Any time you invest emotion in a future, you risk mourning the loss of that future.

When a relationship ends, take time to recover. Allow yourself to grieve and learn what you can from the experience. As you move forward, remember not to rush. It might be soothing to fill the void with another person, but it inhibits real healing, which must happen before you can move forward.

SELF-VALUING TIPS

- Don't let society or social media's filtered version of life tell you what love should look like

- Don't waste your time around people who make you feel bad about yourself, even if they're family or "friends"

- Never settle for less than what you wanted for yourself, but remember "different" is not always "less"

- Don't be afraid to be single – it doesn't mean you're unlovable; it just means you're not rushing

- Surround yourself with positive influences and spend time with people who uplift you

- Engage in hobbies and activities you enjoy to boost your mood and self-esteem

- Embrace failures and setbacks as learning opportunities and use them to gain insight, make improvements, and develop your resilience

- Recognize your strengths, talents, and achievements, and celebrate even your smallest victories, as they contribute to your growth and progress

Without real healing,
you'll carry that pain into
your future relationships,
subconsciously blaming
new partners for the crimes
of the former partner.
If you find yourself still
struggling with relationship
pain or trauma or entering
unhealthy relationships, you
might need more time to
return to the vibrant person
you were before.

CHAPTER 4

Reject Toxic Love

L ove is a truly beautiful thing that makes life worth living, but you have to watch out for imitations. Toxic relationships come disguised as love in the beginning. Under the mask, they're just a breeding ground for pain, manipulation, and abuse.

Real love is built on respect, trust, compassion, and reciprocity. In a healthy relationship, both partners respect each other's boundaries and strive to make each other happy. Love empowers you to grow, thrive, and become the best version of yourself.

Low self-worth gives you rose-colored glasses. Before you ever look for love or even allow love to enter your life, it's vital that you take the time to develop healthy self-worth and learn to identify signs that a person isn't ready for a healthy relationship or simply isn't compatible with what you want for your life.

"If it walks like a duck and quacks like a duck... it's a duck." You don't have to be a duck expert to apply this logic. Anyone can say pretty words and be convincing. Their actions over time – not just during a good phase – will reveal their motivations and priorities.

"Red flag" is a common term for warning signs that potential partners sometimes give in the early stages of dating. People generally try to prevent an attractive version of themselves, so when these red flags pop up, it's wise to pay attention and understand what they might indicate.

For example, controlling behavior or constant criticism in the early days is a red flag. If they're willing to behave that way early on, you're going to see much worse as they get more comfortable and the ease with which you can step away wanes. The red flag in this case can even be as subtle as a noticeable lack of empathy or some belittling comments.

It's not just your partner who might have red flags. Being self-aware and checking your own behavior can also save you from a toxic relationship. You may knowingly or unknowingly exhibit patterns of behavior that tarnish the relationship and create a toxic environment.

Feeling overly jealous, highly dependent, or willing to accept mistreatment are all warning signs on your end. Honest reflection and therapy are powerful tools for addressing your own red flags and preparing you for a healthy relationship in the future.

It's best to take this time for healing and growth on your own, but in some rare cases, a compassionate partner can offer support through the process. This is only advisable if the partner understands what you're struggling with and is otherwise fully compatible with the person you're striving to become. Between the two of you, emotional intelligence, including maturity and self-regulation, needs to be quite high for this to work, and communication must be honest and open, even during difficult conversations.

Recognizing potential indicators of toxic love (red flags) is not about placing blame or passing judgment. The person who is toxic to you might be compatible with someone else, or their toxicity might come from past trauma. Recognizing red flags is only about maintaining healthy boundaries, asserting your needs and expectations, and making the right decisions for your well-being.

Three Scenarios

1 You've been dating a great guy for a few months now. He's handsome, respectful, and seems loyal, but part of you wants to cut the relationship off because he's in a lower income bracket than you are.

2 You're on a first date. The conversation has been easy and lighthearted so far, but you're starting to get more personal. He just finished telling you about his professional ambitions at

work. As you tell him about your own ambitions and fears, he gives short, vague responses, looks around the room, and focuses on his food. You're pretty sure he's not listening to anything you're saying.

3 You've been single for years. You work at home and spend your free time reading, jogging, trying new foods, and watching your favorite TV shows. You love your life, but you worry sometimes that you're getting older and should be building a life with someone by now.

You can probably identify the red flag in scenario #2. The man seems happy to talk about himself but uninterested in learning about you. He doesn't even feign interest. This is a reliable indication that your interests, thoughts, feelings, priorities, and concerns will be openly disregarded in the future.

The other two scenarios describe situations in which you are displaying the red flag. In scenario #1, you obviously value ambition and financial security or freedom. It's great to have your own values and stick by them, but the boyfriend in this scenario doesn't seem to share those values, so the relationship is not viable.

The third scenario is a little harder. This is an independent, happy woman who is not desperate for love. Sounds great, right? The problem is that she wants love to fall into her lap, but she's not putting herself in a position to meet people who share her values and interests. There's a big middle ground between actively seeking love and keeping yourself withdrawn.

There's no way to list all the red flags you might encounter in yourself or in a partner, but you're equipped with a sharp and invaluable tool – intuition. You have an innate ability to know when something is wrong. Don't ignore your intuition. Even if you can't figure out exactly what's raising your alarms, if you know something is off, trust your gut.

What if your relationship is toxic?

If it's a brand-new relationship, you can assess the weight and consistency of the red flags and choose to leave. If you're already in a toxic relationship, it's not so simple.

Start by taking some time to yourself to take a deep breath and assess things objectively. Recognize the emotions you're experiencing and allow them to pass through you. Don't cling to the pain but acknowledge that these are the feelings your relationship is causing you right now.

In a space and time that's free of distraction, assess your self-worth. How you treat yourself dictates how others are allowed to treat you. When you have standards for how you treat yourself, you can easily recognize when other people are failing to meet those standards. Assert your boundaries firmly to yourself and be prepared to assert them to your partner when the time comes.

Once you have a clear view of the situation, and you know what requirements must be met for this relationship to continue, schedule a time to discuss things with your partner. Scheduling time with your partner ensures that there are no distractions and that everyone has time to listen.

Often, the partners in these situations refuse to listen when you bring them your concerns. Do your best to communicate clearly without raised emotions. Avoid verbal attacks. If they try to steer the conversation in a different direction, reiterate the topic and state plainly that this needs to be addressed if you're going to stay in this relationship.

As soon as anyone expresses negative emotion physically, leave the situation immediately.

If the communication is not successful, or if you can't come to a resolution that makes each partner feel heard, validated, and hopeful for the future, take time alone to plan your exit. At this point, the relationship is not viable. Don't emotionally blackmail your partner with a threat to leave. Just take the time you need to accept that this situation is not healthy for anyone and won't provide a happy future and make a detailed plan for yourself.

If it's safe to do so, share your plans with your partner. This is not an appropriate time to discuss solutions. This conversation should take place when you've exhausted your attempts to reconcile. Now, you just need to communicate your intent and give your partner the space to deal with their emotions.

Don't be afraid to walk away from a toxic relationship. Know that you're not mourning the loss of what you have. You're mourning the loss of what you wanted, but what you wanted is still out there for you. You'll never get it if you stay in this toxic situation. It takes strength and courage and self-love to put your well-being first, but it's worth it. Surround yourself with family, friends, and professionals who can help you heal.

Healing will take time. Forgiveness doesn't come all at once. Be patient with yourself. Don't rush. While you get used to being single again, identify behaviors and areas of your life you can improve upon, and put your focus there. Refuse to blame yourself for the failure of the relationship, and remember you are worthy of love and happiness.

CHAPTER 5

7 Pillars of Healthy Love

Healthy love – comforting love that has longevity, intimacy, and equality – is built on strong values. Most relationships don't start out with all the pillars standing firmly in place, but a viable love will have the capacity to develop what's missing through loving, respectful cooperation and compatibility.

These are the core values that healthy love is built upon:

Equality

Healthy love grows on a foundation of equality and balance. From the very beginning, if both partners don't feel equal, the dynamic won't flow comfortably with respect on both sides. Healthy love does not put one person in a superior, dominating, or controlling role.

Equality and balance don't mean every single decision will be made together. It's nice to be able to hand responsibility to another person sometimes, but they need to be able to hand responsibility back to you. If someone struggles to relinquish control or struggles to accept control, one or both parties will start to feel overburdened and unappreciated or invalidated and undervalued.

Support

Healthy love is inherently supportive because the two of you care deeply about one another and want to make each other happy. It should feel comfortable and natural to give and receive support without fear of being taken for granted, belittled, or hurt. Your partner should be your biggest cheerleader, offering emotional support, encouragement, and a helping hand when needed.

You should do the same. Healthy love is a give-and-take, not a give-and-give-and-give. It's a partnership in which you can feel secure knowing they have your back, and you have theirs, no matter what challenges you face together.

Communication

A relationship cannot be healthy and fulfilling without communication. Transparency, respect, and compromise are vital aspects of sharing your life with another person. For love to be healthy, you must feel safe expressing your feelings.

Your partner must be able to listen to understand, not to defend, dismiss, or divert. When your partner talks to you, you must offer the same support. In this dynamic, both parties feel heard, validated, satisfied, and more connected after communicating with each other.

Being open and vulnerable is the only way to build a rock-solid foundation that lasts a lifetime. Healthy communication fosters a deeper sense of intimacy, trust, and love. That makes all the difference between a successful relationship and a relationship that crashes and burns – or slowly suffocates you over time.

Respect

Respect should never – ever – be absent from a relationship. It should start the moment you meet each other and never wane. Even in times of disagreement, moodiness, stress, and anger, your partner should value your opinion, honor your boundaries, treasure your individuality, and care for your feelings. If your relationship does not have respect, your relationship does not exist.

There will be hurtful comments and actions. Human beings are imperfect. Despite the strongest love, you and your partner might sometimes say things you don't mean and do things you regret. If there's no pattern, and the disrespect doesn't cross zero-tolerance boundaries (abuse, cheating, etc.), those moments can be overcome with healthy communication, sincere remorse, and forgiveness.

Trust

Your relationship is meant to be a secure environment where you can be authentic, vulnerable, and safe. That level of complete security requires real trust – not the kind of trust that says, "I'm pretty sure he won't let me down," but the kind that says, "He won't let me down. He never would."

Having faith in your partner's actions, words, and integrity allows you to thrive as a couple, but you don't – and shouldn't – trust someone that deeply overnight. It takes time and consistent honesty, reliability, and effective communication.

When most people think about trust in a relationship, they think about fidelity. Fidelity should be the most basic and reliable type of trust between you and your partner. There should be no question that they're choosing you every day.

Lifelong love requires trust that transcends all levels. If you were on life support, would you trust your partner with power of attorney? Would you know in your soul that he would make the right decisions with your life, your children, and your assets?

Vulnerability

We keep a lot of ourselves under wraps. There are characteristics that are seen as unattractive or undesirable in women, so we don't show those bits. Some of us have been so hurt in the past that we hide the parts of ourselves that are more susceptible to that pain.

Many of us hide behind a brave and seemingly confident exterior. Whatever you have to do to feel safe in the outside world, you should never have to hide from your partner.

Your partner is your safe place, even more so than when you're alone. You should be able to be yourself, not the version of yourself that you think they want to see. No act. No bravery. All the so-called "ugly" or "boring" parts of you should be loved the same as the rest. Your partner shouldn't welcome toxic behaviors with a smile, but we're all hard to love sometimes. They should love your real self with compassion and understanding.

Friendship

If your partner is not your friend, your relationship has an expiration date. Relationships tend to have seasons. Passion, excitement, and intimacy can fade at times. Friendship is what keeps you together. If you can't simply enjoy their company without romance, you should evaluate your compatibility and the viability of your relationship.

There's a reason strong couples will often say, "He or she is my best friend." Genuinely liking each other as individuals creates an unshakable sense of companionship, which is a critical part of feeling fulfilled as a person. A relationship built on true friendship is unmatched.

CHAPTER 6

Communicating with Men

The world likes to say women are complicated, but men are quite the enigma themselves. Understanding the intricacies of the male psyche and decoding their thoughts and emotions feels like driving a car blindfolded.

Like women, every man is an individual with his own experiences and personality. Generalizing will cause you to misunderstand and potentially alienate your partner. You can't map out their every thought on paper, but a sincere effort to understand your partner as a unique individual will help them feel secure and fulfilled in your relationship. That security improves your dynamic and the longevity of your life together.

The common generalization is that men are simple, emotionless creatures while women are vastly complicated, emotional overthinkers. Both sides of this coin lower standards of behavior and compassion, prevent women from being taken seriously, and place a painful – and sometimes dangerous – pressure on men to withhold emotions that are inaccurately labeled as delicate or feminine.

Everyone is born with the same potential range of emotion, barring some atypical conditions. If you enter the situation with that understanding, you're more likely to listen for comprehension. Your partner will only be open with you if you provide a judgment-free environment in which they feel safe being vulnerable.

Judgment is an automatic human reaction to all new stimuli. You can change those automatic thoughts and opinions by improving your understanding and consciously practicing empathy and appreciation for their honesty. This opens the door for a genuine connection. However, this acceptance does not extend to toxic behaviors.

ASK YOURSELF

1. Am I receptive when he tries to open up?
2. Do I close my mouth and listen so he can express himself?
3. Do I offer him support and encouragement?
4. Do I show judgment?
5. Am I emotionally available to him?
6. Do I show my appreciation when he opens up to me?

In a healthy relationship with effective communication, you both need the emotional intelligence to verbally express your feelings with clarity and accuracy. Much of the time, partners are almost there, but they need a little support and encouragement from one another to find the right words, clarify their feelings, and reach a fulfilling resolution for both people.

If one person can't express their emotions intelligently and doesn't work with their partner to improve understanding, both parties will carry the heavy burden of all the feelings they can't share with each other. Bitterness will germinate, and the relationship will fail.

You and your partner will likely have different communication styles, on top of any stereotyping and societal pressure. Depending on your partner's disposition, it might be difficult to wade through the delivery to appreciate the message.

One of you might be more direct than the other, which can feel offensive to someone more sensitive. One of you might be more long-winded, which can make it harder for the recipient to understand the root of the message. Take things slow and know that being honest is not the same as deliberately hurting you. Ask for clarification when you don't understand and be patient when they don't understand.

Men seek love, validation, and meaningful connection, just like women. An emotionally healthy man in a healthy relationship will tell you when something is wrong before it creates a rift. He'll work with you to resolve issues and be available to listen to your concerns. He'll take criticism without defensively derailing the conversation and won't lash out at others in anger or frustration.

Practice empathy and appreciation for your partner's vulnerability. Let him know you're listening and that you won't judge him for sharing with you. Offer words of affirmation, even if he doesn't show that he needs them. Over time, he'll develop trust in the safe space you're creating, and your communication will improve.

CHAPTER 7

Climbing the Ladder

T he ladder to success feels more like a rope. It takes every ounce of your strength and determination to pull yourself up, only to discover a ceiling that says, "This is as high as a woman can go."

It's no secret that we face barriers unique to our sex in career advancement. If you're entry-level, your boss could be a woman, and she worked damn hard to get there. But her boss? A man. And his boss? A man. And that man's boss? No question. That's a man.

If there's a token female executive in the C-suite, it's because the company actively practices Diversity, Equity, and Inclusion so they can check the box next to "corporate social responsibility" in the marketing notebook. It's probably safe to assume she struggles to be taken seriously or effect any real action within the company.

The difficulty we face in professional advancement places a stigma on women who have advanced further than what's typical.

It's often said that those women have leveraged non-professional assets – those unique to women – to get to where they are now.

The reality is that it's much more common for men in positions of authority to proposition, harass, or assault ambitious female subordinates without reciprocation. Those women often tolerate the abuse without participating or sacrifice their positions to preserve their integrity.

If you haven't faced this behavior already, statistics show that you probably will at some point. Over 77% of women are verbally harassed at work. More than half are touched without consent.

It's important to remember that your response will help shape the future landscape for women in the workplace. Devaluing yourself for professional gain is the worst possible choice you could make. The emotional repercussions can be severe. The damage to your reputation will be irreversible.

There's always the chance that you won't achieve any professional gain at all, but even if you do, it will be at the expense of other women… and yourself. We've fought tirelessly for generations to achieve equality and recognition. The only way up is to uphold the principles that have paved the way. Gender-based biases and abuses are disheartening, but shortcuts undermine our entire collective effort.

The best choice you could make in this situation is to gather evidence and report to HR or the police, whichever is appropriate, as soon as possible. This course of action will likely be detrimental to your career, but it will help hold abusive leaders accountable and change the way women are viewed and treated at work. It's a step we must take to change the world.

You possess all the skills and qualities needed for success. You're sharp, analytical, communicative, hungry, and a born leader. You know what you want, and you're going to get it. You never have to devalue yourself or allow others to downplay your competence.

This would only confirm their suspicion that you don't deserve to be there. Be confident in your abilities and what you bring to the table. Don't sacrifice your values. If you don't see your worth, no one else will see it either.

When I was young, my parents told me I could be anything I wanted to be, if I worked hard and performed well in school. As I got older, they advised me to aim for female-friendly careers. I still hear parents giving the same advice to their daughters today.

If you've never heard it, it's hard to imagine someone saying such an offensive thing, but once you enter the workforce and encounter the female reality, you realize those words were meant with love and protection. Misguided as they were, my parents knew what I would face and didn't want me to struggle for work.

We've come a long way since then, but not far enough. For most of us today, our dreams will only ever be dreams. The battlefield is vast and treacherous. We'll only make it if we continue to support each other.

How many women have you elevated on your journey to success? What can you do to break the ceiling for yourself and others? These are the questions we must ask ourselves. It's not about me or you. It's about women. We must take conscious strides together to change the way the world looks at us.

Mentorship programs, networking initiatives, resources, and support systems empower women to surpass their perceived limitations. Wherever you are on the ladder, you can help another woman, even just by joining a group or being a friend.

CHAPTER 8

Competition

There's another generalization about women that's hard to deny. Almost all of us have experienced it. Women are seen as jealous, catty, petty, and conniving. The unfortunate reality is that many of us tear each other down out of insecurity.

Jealousy is a natural human emotion that we all feel now and then. It stems from insecurity, fear, and feelings of inadequacy. We've become so accustomed to fighting for opportunities that, when we see another woman succeed, our feelings of inadequacy intensify. Jealousy becomes an ugly monster in the worst possible moments.

How we deal with moments of jealousy is what matters. Instead of allowing it to consume you, contaminate your good nature, and influence your behavior, take a moment to assess what you're feeling and why.

Are you fulfilled? Are your relationships and your job secure? Do you regret choices or have trauma from events in your past?

Is there something about yourself that you want to change? Your success is unique to who you are. You have your own path to walk. Another woman's success, luck, or happiness will not get in your way, but a lack of confidence and security could.

As you develop your self-worth, you'll suffer fewer and less intense jealous moments. Though the inadequacy mindset is a fierce opponent, you can take action to improve your self-image and view others in a healthy light.

How to Feel Adequate

1 Consciously acknowledge and celebrate your strengths, talents, and accomplishments. Celebrate your victories out loud, no matter how small. Instead of looking at where you are compared to other people, look at how far you've come from where you started.

2 Banish comparisons. All the images of perfection and success in your life are there for one purpose – to sell you something. These are deliberately unattainable standards, and they will steal your joy if you let them. Focus on your own goals and progress. Celebrate your growth and achievement. If your goal is someone else's version of perfection, you will always be disappointed.

3 Take care of yourself physically and mentally. Prioritize yourself at least once a day to take stock of your emotional

and physical well-being and do something that makes you feel happy and healthy. Self-care is just as important as the care you devote to everything else.

4 Build a reliable support network. No matter how strong you are, you cannot survive this life alone. Everyone needs affirmation and support from people who genuinely care about them. Without that, human beings don't just lose confidence or get lonely; we can suffer real, clinical mental disturbances.

5 Practice gratitude. Why do we say, "Practice gratitude" instead of simply, "Be grateful?" When you practice gratitude, you're not just grateful for something. You actively, consciously reflect on the positives in your life. Some days, you'll feel like your only positive is that the sun was shining, but taking just a second to acknowledge it will train your brain to recognize positives on a regular basis.

Uplifting other women is not just a noble act; it's an investment in our collective success. Let's celebrate our victories and share in each other's joy. Cheer each other on with words of encouragement so that you may hear words of encouragement instead of sneers when you're the one in the spotlight. We gain nothing by tearing each other down, but we have a lot to gain by being kind.

Sarah

In a perfect world, we would be each other's cheerleaders and allies, but we've been conditioned by society to always be in heavy competition with each other. We've been told there isn't room at the top for women and that the gift of men's affection relies on our ability to beat out the other girl, so our instinct tells us to drag others down for self-preservation.

Sarah recently started a job at a prestigious marketing firm. She rose quickly up the ranks because of her bold creativity and serious work ethic. She got results that helped renew client contracts and received recognition for her contributions to the company.

People who had been at the firm much longer than Sarah started to feel cheated. Jealousy crept through the office, and people were soon gossiping about Sarah, how she had moved up so quickly, and why she received so much praise.

One woman was quite bitter. She had been striving for promotion for over three years with little response or encouragement from her superiors. Her gossip turned to vicious character assassination. She told multiple people that she suspected Sarah of sleeping with her supervisor.

Other jealous coworkers were quick to latch on to the lies, spreading rumors and undermining Sarah's credibility. It made everyone feel better, momentarily, to think that Sarah wasn't better at the job than they were; she just had an unfair advantage.

It wasn't long before Sarah heard the rumors herself. She could tell that most of her coworkers had become less amiable over the past weeks. There was a negative energy around her, with the occasional sideways glance and whispers.

Fortunately for Sarah, her go-getter personality helped her be resilient and less susceptible to this kind of immature behavior. She was hurt, as anyone would be when they discover they're disliked by people in their lives, but she refused to engage and focused on her work instead.

The office leadership became aware of the situation and HR was involved. They learned that the bitter woman was the source of the inappropriate conversation, and she was fired from the firm. The response might not have been so harsh, but Sarah had already been offered a supervisory position in the office, and HR decided the office culture would be better without that strenuous dynamic.

Most of us would have unpleasant feelings if a new person came into our office and immediately surpassed us, but had the woman made a conscious decision to be positive, she could have learned from Sarah, built a supportive dynamic, and ended up with a boss who was invested in her success.

You might not relate to the office scenario, but you can probably think of a time you heard false rumors about yourself. You probably know by now that the best response to that situation is to not engage. And if you've ever found yourself saying ugly and unfounded things about another woman, you can probably look back and see that those comments came from a place of insecurity inside you.

The next time you're presented with negative feelings towards another woman or another woman's negative feelings towards you, try to be objective and assess where those feelings are coming from. Remember not to allow other people to rob you of your positivity, supportive attitude, and future opportunities.

Ignore the noise,
stay focused,
and let your
hard work
speak for you.

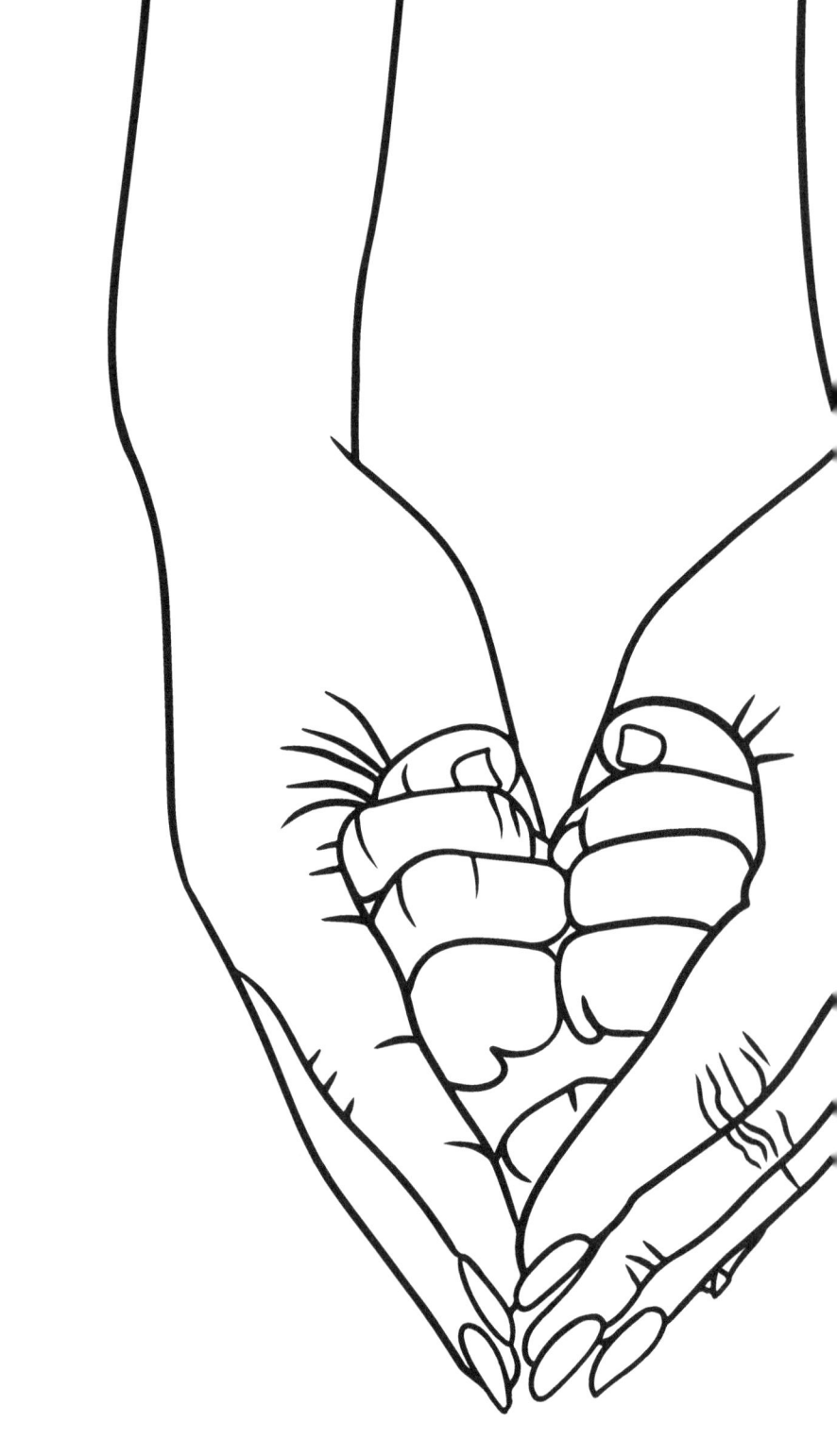

CHAPTER 9

What's a mom?

Motherhood is the most fun, hard, and rewarding challenge you'll face in your life, if it's something you want for yourself. It comes with relentless pressure, unrealistic expectations, constant overwhelm, and inconceivable joy.

Social media will make you feel like garbage all the time. (The best thing you can do for yourself – and maybe your child – is to get rid of it.) Every perfect mom will remind you that you're dropping the ball again. They have perfect lives, husbands, children, homes, skin, hair, and bodies, and wouldn't be caught dead underdressed or without makeup at Target.

Those perfect moms don't exist. They're made-up characters. The real perfect mom does exist, and she's more common than any type of influencer or content creator. She doesn't always have perfect skin and manicured nails, and she probably doesn't have a social media following. She's fiercely protective, loves her children desperately, and could use a few more hours of sleep.

Real motherhood is messy, chaotic, and beautifully imperfect. It's full of sleepless nights, diaper explosions, tantrums, teenage angst, tears, fear, guilt, and love. You balance the different parts of your lives as best as you can and hope for the best.

This chapter is dedicated to you – the perfect mother. Here, we celebrate your superpowers of strength, resilience, and serious multitasking. If you haven't taken a moment today to assess what YOU need – and we know you haven't – let's do that here now.

Support Network

There's nothing better than a healthy support network. It's a complicated part of caring for yourself, and it's just as vital as eating or sleeping. False friends and family members who bring you down are like quicksand on your path. They slow you down, disrupt your peace, and fill you with fear and doubt.

Trusted friends, a loving family, other moms, and professionals fill your fearful moments with guidance, confidence, and direction. If you don't have anyone like this in your life, check out some local online groups where moms and other women empower one another.

Time Management

If you struggle with time management, you know exactly how valuable it is – or at least how valuable it would be if you could get the hang of it. When your time is unmanaged, you constantly feel like there aren't enough hours in the day, like your to-do list grows faster than you can cross things off.

You don't have to be a robot and burn through tasks with laser focus. You just have to set priorities and boundaries and create a schedule that accommodates your professional and personal duties while leaving room for life. You must know when to say "no," when to delegate, and how to be realistic about your time frames.

Self-Care

Self-care isn't a luxury. It's essential to the mental and physiological well-being of every person on the planet. When you take care of yourself, you can be fully present in your work and home life. You can give your best because you feel your best.

Make time for activities that recharge your batteries. Whatever makes you feel relaxed, happy, and healthy can be a self-care activity. Reading, yoga, bathing, medication, mindful rest, walking, working out, hobbies, friends… you need a moment of self-renewal every single day.

Sleep

You cannot pour from an empty cup. Taking care of yourself – which includes at least seven hours of uninterrupted sleep every night – allows you to show up as the best you for your children and the people who rely on you.

A lack of sleep can make even the strongest mother break down. A well-rested mom is better equipped to handle the challenges of parenting. If you have a baby who doesn't sleep through the night yet, do your best and get help when you need it, even if it's just for a nap here and there. If your kids are older and you have the opportunity to get the rest you need, take it.

Your health depends largely on your sleep patterns, and your family and work depend on your health. It's not selfish. It's not lazy. Get some sleep, so you can live your life and be as great as you were meant to be.

Guilt

There's hardly a woman in the world who doesn't have guilt over something. Every mom has parenting guilt. Working moms have parenting guilt that extends to their performance at work because that work directly contributes to their children's quality of life, but it also detracts from family life.

You're not spending enough time with your family. You're not giving your best at work. You missed another event. You were too harsh. You were too soft. You're not taking care of yourself. Your "me time" is selfish. It's a never-ending cycle.

The truth is that you are phenomenal. Even on the days when

you don't do your best, when you know you could have done better but you just didn't, even on those days, you are more than enough. You're setting an incredible example of dedication, sacrifice, and hard work. Cherish the moments you have with your children, and they'll cherish them too.

Flexibility

Flexibility helps the different parts of your life run smoothly, and it's not just you. You need a flexible network too. Seek employers and opportunities that offer flexibility in scheduling and duties. Keep your schedule semi-fluid. Being more relaxed about who has to be where at what time will alleviate some of the pressure of work-life-kids-relationship-self integrations.

Communication

Be transparent with your family and employer about your needs and availability. Explore strategies together to achieve success in both realms. Communicate with everyone about commitments and involve them in your process of finding balance and understanding. This can also help you identify weaknesses in your network that cause unnecessary stress. Pay attention to anyone who resists your attempts to communicate and work effectively together.

Not a mother?

You might be thinking, "I don't even have kids. You're not talking to me," but I am. We have a gift of nurture that extends beyond the traditional role of motherhood. Whether we have children or not, most of us are programmed with this drive to care for all the people around us before ourselves.

If you have pets, volunteer at a shelter or home, help care for family members, nurture your partner, or share your heart in any way, this is for you.

It's a wonderful person who cares deeply about those around her, but the facts still stand. You MUST take care of yourself if you want to be effective. Your natural inclination to provide comfort, guidance, and support must include yourself.

CHAPTER 10

Superwoman Syndrome

E xpectation is a heavy burden. Against all logic, we've somehow reached a point where we're expected to handle every aspect of life in the developed world, but we're also undervalued, underestimated, and dismissed in professional – and even personal – settings.

We're seen as weak and expected to be strong. We're seen as simple and expected to manage complex logistics and operations. We're seen as emotional and expected to handle everything without being overwhelmed or feeling hurt so that no one cares how hard we're working. Our workload is viewed as manageable, even easy, no matter how big it gets.

It's the curse of being the Superwoman. If you've ever seen a comic book or superhero show, you're probably familiar with this story. The public and the police label the hero a villain or a criminal because a car or a building was damaged. Forget about the hundreds of lives or even the entire world that they saved. No matter how many plates you're spinning, most people will only see the one that falls.

How many times this week have you thought, "I'm tired," without saying anything out loud or taking any action to get some rest? You probably looked at the clock and told yourself, "That's okay. It's already 2 PM. I can probably go to sleep in… 10 hours."

Our society glorifies productivity. We're conditioned to believe that only the weak or lazy get tired, so we push forward no matter how high the toll on our well-being. Regardless of the cost to our performance, patience, and mental health, "rest" and "tired" are banished from our vocabularies.

Alexa, play *Superwoman* by Alecia Keys.

Gabrielle

Gabrielle wakes up at 4 AM every day for a workout. Then she takes a quick shower and packs well-planned lunches for her three kids and husband. She gets herself ready for work, and at 6 AM, she gently wakes everyone up and helps them prepare for the day ahead.

When everyone is ready, Gabrielle says goodbye to her husband, loads the kids into the car, and takes them to two different schools before going to work. Her husband picks them up from school because she works well into the evening most days.

When Gabrielle gets home, she immediately makes dinner because everyone is hungry. After dinner, she gets the kids through their bathing routines and ready for bed one by one. If it's not 9 PM yet, she'll spend a little quality time with her family before the kids go to sleep. She usually has no energy left to spend time with her husband after that.

At first glance, this sounds like an efficiently run household, but this kind of schedule isn't sustainable. Gabrielle is consistently not getting enough sleep, and there's no flexibility in her day to breathe, relax, and reenergize herself.

Gabrielle is a victim of superwoman syndrome. Her self-care is neglected, and she is fast approaching the point of total burnout. Her husband's domestic duties are limited to picking up the kids, leaving the weight of the household to fall heavy on Gabrielle's shoulders.

Women like Gabrielle often end up wondering why they feel empty, anxious, and without direction in their lives. They have no opportunity for personal growth, relaxation, and the development of relationships. She can't see the obvious problems because she doesn't have five minutes for reflection. She has no hobbies, and her quality time with her loved ones is rushed and limited.

Asking for help and admitting your fatigue are not shameful actions. Just like every other physical and emotional need, our bodies and minds require regular rest and relief. If anything in Gabrielle's situation is shameful, it's that her husband hasn't realized the unequal burden on his wife.

The common expectation for women to shoulder the lion's share of domestic and personal responsibilities in addition to their fair share of professional responsibility is antiquated. We accept it because it's easier. We're agreeable, and we believe it when we're told we should be able to do this without a problem.

Some of us are addicted to the need to please everyone, which typically comes from chronic childhood trauma. We're afraid to disappoint anyone or in desperate need of approval, so we say "yes" to every request and destroy ourselves on the quest to meet everyone else's needs.

Saying "no" doesn't make you selfish. It makes you a real person with needs and limitations, and "no" doesn't always have to be harsh. You can admit that you can't accommodate a specific request and offer an alternative that aligns with your availability, capability, values, and priorities. Not everyone will respond with emotional maturity, and that's okay.

Getting out from under this expectation starts with reinforcing your boundaries and your expectations of the people in your life who are supposed to be sharing the load. Erase your schedule and start from scratch, prioritizing your well-being and happiness without guilt. As you make space for yourself in your life, you'll feel more balanced and fulfilled, and you'll have the clarity to identify your path.

You are a strong, intelligent, and highly capable human being, not an invincible mythical creature that never breaks a sweat. You're not Babe the Blue Ox, waiting for the great Paul Bunyan's next command. You will continue to accomplish great things while you take care of yourself, and they'll feel even more rewarding than before.

CHAPTER 11

I was talking.

E very self-help and personal development book has a section on speaking. It is the most ignored advice by far, but it's worth repeating again and again. Your voice deserves to be heard. It has the power to change lives. Being a woman doesn't mean you have little to contribute.

We hesitate to express our thoughts for fear of rejection and judgment. Our voices aren't as loud as the others in the room, so we must speak up. We must be clear, calm, confident, and impassable. Not walked on or spoken over. Easier said than done.

When a man is assertive, even blunt, he's respected for it. A woman saying the same words would appear emotional and argumentative. In a professional setting, you could lose your upward mobility completely. In some cases, your superiors might even rethink your ability to handle the pressures of your current position.

Your friends, family, and strangers on the street do things that warrant a response every day. You're called to advocate for yourself, stand up for what's right, be a champion for justice, and challenge the status quo.

You want to speak up, but you know you'll be drawing bias and judgment the second you call attention to yourself in a way that's not overly agreeable and pleasant. The good news is that a stronger voice can cut through some of that misperception just by being strong.

Changing the way your voice rings out in the spaces you occupy starts with self-discovery. Take time to reflect on your values. What is important to you besides other people? What are your passions and beliefs? When you know yourself well, it's easier to express your thoughts and opinions with conviction, and it's easier to admit when you need more information or time to consider something.

You'll still encounter a world of bias, but it won't be able to hold you down. The biggest indicators of success are grit and determination, openness and extroversion, and conscientiousness. Give yourself a voice, take pride in your work, and don't let anyone stop you.

These exercises can help you develop an external voice that others will listen to:

Voice Journaling

Grab your journal and open the voice memo recorder on your phone. Take a deep breath, press the record button, and talk. It doesn't matter what you say. Talk about your day or what you're thinking about right now. The point is just to get comfortable saying what's in your head.

When you feel like you've gotten the hang of recording yourself, start a new recording and talk about your goals and dreams. Share your recent challenges and accomplishments. At the end, give yourself a positive affirmation.

When you're done, listen to both recordings. Think about how it feels to hear your own voice. How does it feel to hear yourself speak your struggles and aspirations aloud? As you listen, write your thoughts in your journal.

For best results, use daily.

Mirror Talk

Prepare a few affirmations and positive messages for yourself. Stand in front of a mirror, look yourself in the eye, and speak your messages clearly and confidently. Remind yourself of the qualities you love about yourself and use positive self-talk to address the things you don't like.

You might feel silly at first, but the more you practice, the more confident you'll become. Over time, you'll notice the confidence you manifest for the mirror stays with you throughout the day, and your self-image becomes more positive.

Debate Club

Debating is a great way to break out of your comfort zone and get yourself talking. There aren't many adult debate clubs available these days. See if you can find something locally or online. Debate club activities will sharpen your critical thinking skills and help you articulate your argument with logical reasoning. These tools will give you the confidence to express your opinions in real-life situations.

Toastmasters

Toastmasters is a nonprofit organization that helps individuals improve their public speaking and leadership skills. People from diverse backgrounds get together to practice communication and other relevant skills and share constructive feedback to help each other improve. If Toastmasters isn't available in your area, look for another speaking club that offers similar activities.

Assertiveness Practice

If you struggle to maintain your boundaries, express your needs, and address your concerns in a group setting, this exercise is for you. There are many exercises you can research to improve your assertiveness. We'll start with saying "no."

When a topic arises that is at odds with your boundaries or needs, mentally prepare yourself to calmly say "no." Express your boundaries clearly, respectfully, and firmly, using "I" statements. Use active listening to understand the argument being offered, and if that argument doesn't warrant the violation of your boundary, say "no."

Remember assertiveness is not aggressive or dismissive. It is simply the firm establishment of your needs.

CHAPTER 12

Fertility and Femininity

F ertility is a quality bestowed in a seemingly random fashion. Some women go their whole lives without really thinking about their fertility or what it is to be a woman. Others shed endless tears over the absence of this simple functionality that is so synonymous with femininity. Some choose not to have children and then face the condescension of a world that expects women to be mothers.

Infertility

The ability to conceive, carry, and deliver a child is taken for granted by almost everyone who has done it or plans to do it without difficulty or complication. We're all joyful and grateful for our children, but we often forget what a miracle it is that we could begin that journey in the first place.

Wondering whether you'll be able to have a child or learning definitively that you can't causes very real grief. You grieve the loss of your dreams for the future. Whether you've been dreaming of that child your whole life or just recently, your baby is a deeply embedded hope that cannot be painlessly removed.

Grief is better managed with a healthy support system, but with infertility, you suffer a type of emotional isolation. The societal expectation is that you'll graduate, get a job, marry a man, and have children. The world doesn't understand when you don't or can't.

Even those closest to you will say all the wrong things and give you gifts like fertility oil and positive affirmation socks, as if hope and gimmicks will evaporate your medical condition. It's embarrassing to talk about, and no one gets it anyway, so you suffer in silence.

Infertility becomes part of your ego at the expense of your sense of femininity. Women have babies. Healthy, desirable, feminine women are fertile. They're mothers. They facilitate fatherhood for their partners. They don't go to the doctor every week for shots. They don't have a calendar dedicated to a complicated schedule of medical procedures. They're not empty shells. If you can't be a mother, are you even a woman?

Your path to motherhood is part of your unique path through life. It's not going to look like everyone else's, and there's nothing wrong or even strange about that. Women are not carbon-copied one after the other. We're each made up of a multitude of experiences, abilities, and potential beyond reproduction. Your femininity is not defined by your ability to conceive.

This part of your journey is monumental. It influences your entire future, but it does not make or break your worth and womanhood. Allow your grief to take up space in your chest. Allow your circle to love and support you, even if they don't really get it. Find a group or counselor with insight. Make your world a safe space to experience your feelings, where you don't always have to explain yourself.

Individuality

If you tell someone you plan to buy a condo in a couple of years, they'll probably say something like, "Oh, that's great," or, "Why a condo instead of a house?" If you explain your preference for an urban environment and low-maintenance property, they'll probably say something like, "Well, that sounds great. Can't wait to see your new place." You wouldn't expect them to say, "You think you want a condo now, but you'll change your mind when you get older."

Some women, especially older and more traditional women, cannot imagine a young woman not dreaming of becoming a mother. At one point, the quintessence of the female experience was a suburban home with a hard-working husband and two or three children to care for as a stay-at-home wife mother.

While that sounds like a beautiful life for someone who wants it, it's not ideal for everyone. More and more women today are recognizing their freedom to live a life without kids, and that life is just as valid and meaningful as a life with kids.

Everyone from your closest family member to an unknown old woman at the grocery store will feel comfortable telling you that you don't know what you want, you'll change your mind later, and you just don't understand what you're missing out on.

It's true that motherhood is an inconceivable joy, but that doesn't mean it fits with everyone's dream for their life, and there are a multitude of logical reasons to not bring more children into the world. Regardless of the condescension and judgment you deal with when people learn about your plans, choosing not to have kids is not the same as choosing not to be a woman.

Women are such diverse beings that there isn't a detailed definition of femininity. The dictionary will tell you it's the "traditional qualities associated with womanhood," but we reject this definition because we reject the idea that you aren't feminine if you don't exhibit the "traditional" qualities. You don't have to wear pink bows, flutter your eyelashes shyly at boys, do the dishes, and have children to be a beautiful, powerful, fruitful, feminine woman.

Moving Forward

For whatever reason, you're not having a child the traditional way right now. So, what are you going to do? Those who have chosen this path probably have no problem answering this question because they're already on the path they wanted. For you, all that's left to do is ignore the ignorance of the people who try to tell you what you want and need in your life.

Sidenote: If you ever do decide you want a child, don't hold back just to prove those people wrong. No matter what you do with your life, what they're saying and how they're saying it is wrong. You're in charge of yourself now, and you're in charge of yourself later.

If you ended up in this position because that's what life handed you, maybe it's not so clear. There's no right answer. Your life is still your life, and you can pivot in any direction you choose. When your plans are canceled or postponed, you have to ask yourself what you want to do now.

Take your time, explore your options, and remember that you still exemplify all that is woman. Your perspective, strengths, and impact are invaluable. Have faith and trust that life will continue to blossom for you in many ways.

CHAPTER 13

The Power of Faith

W hen people hear "faith," they typically think "religion," but "faith" has a broader meaning. It's about trust and belief. It's a source of strength, comfort, and hope in difficult times. Faith can be a guiding force that fortifies your resilience and ability to overcome obstacles.

For a lot of people, faith is rooted in religious or spiritual beliefs. Faith can also be a deeply personal internal experience that transcends notions of religion. It can reveal the constant, inherent goodness of humanity, the power of love, and the interconnectedness of all things.

Faith doesn't rid your life of challenges. Everything won't suddenly get easy because you have faith, but a developed faith will help you find meaning and purpose in the blessings and challenges life brings you. Depending on your personal beliefs, it might also help you feel less lonely and more supported in difficult moments.

When we talk about faith and womanhood, it's impossible not to be reminded of incredible women throughout history who have exemplified unwavering belief in something greater than themselves. These remarkable women have left an indelible mark on the world through their achievements and conviction.

One such woman is Rosa Parks. We all know her name because her courageous act of staying in her seat sparked the Montgomery Bus Boycott, a pivotal moment in the Civil Rights Movement. Rosa's faith in justice and equality fueled her legendary determination and significant social change.

A more recent inspiration is Malala Yousafzai. Despite the grave danger, Malala advocates for girls' education in Pakistan. She believes that education is a fundamental right for every child and was awarded the Nobel Peace Prize for her fearless perseverance. She is a global symbol of resilience and hope.

But what about ordinary women like us?

It's easy to overlook the countless women who make a difference in the world every day. Their contributions don't make headlines, but their impact is profound and worthy of recognition. Some stand tall and strong as the backbones of their families, even when they feel like they're falling apart. Some drive the world's expectations of women onward and upward through their relentless conscientiousness in their work.

Operating in these overlooked roles requires faith and a deep understanding of oneself. Most of us move deftly through daily life without much thought of faith or the comfort and strength it can provide. If you're not intimately familiar with personal faith, review the following practices for cultivating more active faith in your daily life. Consider implementing these daily exercises as a starting point for your self-exploration to see the difference faith can make.

Your Values

What matters most to you? What are the principles that guide your choices? Identifying these values and describing them in clear language will help you develop a deeper understanding of your personal belief system.

Mindfulness

Set aside moments of quiet introspection to connect with yourself. Give yourself at least a few minutes of meditation and journaling every day. Be fully present. This concentrated reflection gives you a higher level of clarity, reduces stress, and can even improve your health.

Inspiration and Wisdom

Explore sources of inspiration that resonate with you. Read books, listen to podcasts, attend workshops and talks, engage in conversation with the people around you, expose yourself to different perspectives, and submerge yourself in nature or another environment that moves you.

Acts of Faith

Start with small steps that require trust in something outside yourself. Set an intention, and take a leap towards your goal, trusting the process of life itself. Every small act of trust develops your faith muscles and strengthens your ability to rely on something by faith alone.

Control

Accept that there are things beyond your control. Practice surrendering to the flow of life. Suppress your urge to control every decision and outcome and let things happen, trusting that everything will unfold exactly how it's meant to. Surrendering control makes space for faith to thrive and opens up your world to unexpected blessings.

Cultivating faith is a never-ending personal journey. It takes ongoing patience and practice. Be gentle with yourself as you explore and deepen your faith. Embrace the process and trust that you are where you need to be. As you repeat these practices, you'll discover a greater sense of self and an enhanced ability to stand on your faith.

CHAPTER 14

Enough!

T he world's standards tell us we're inadequate in multiple ways every day. We've all felt at some point or the other like we're not enough. We've all screamed, "I can't do this," whether out loud or inside our heads. Some of us feel it pressing, pulsating, and pounding away at us, while for others it's a faint but constant aching within our souls. The thoughts of not being enough put racing ideas and a myriad of doubts and feelings of utter frustration or conversely, you may have that unyielding desire to push forward, depending on the type of individual that you are. If you are optimistic, half-full type, you will definitely keep it pushing, but if you see the glass half empty all the time, then the opposite is true. Maybe you're thinking it right now.

You started out in life with a long list of hopes and dreams, but along the way, you were repeatedly told you *can't* really have those things because you're not male, beautiful, wealthy, or some other arbitrary quality.

But your worth is not determined by anyone or anything other than you. You set the standards for yourself, and you set the standards for how you're willing to be treated by other people. Your partner, friends and family, coworkers, and the world cannot diminish your worth with their own words and behaviors.

You'll have moments of self-doubt. You'll assess a situation or challenge and question whether you can do it or deserve the thing you want. This is often an issue in relationships, domestics, and careers. When that feeling comes, recognize it, acknowledge that it's a normal type of anxiety, and let it pass right through because you're not going to be scared away from your goals.

You have inherent strength, charm, and the ability to live out your wildest dreams. It's not too hopeful to believe you'll find fulfillment in every aspect of your life. Never forget that you, as you are right now, are enough. You are worthy and capable of love, success, and happiness.

You're a warrior, even in your lowest moments. You can break through or climb over any obstacle that stands in your way. You won't roll over and give up ever again, no matter how many times you've done it in the past. Defeat is not an option, and you will not be swayed.

It's easy to say all of that with confidence right now, but how do you make it feel true when you're beaten down, devastated, or overwhelmed, and everything in your life is telling you you're just not that special person who deserves the special things? How do you feel worthy when all the evidence says you're not worth the loving relationship, the coveted position, the successful business, or the Mother of the Year Award?

It's not easy, but with conviction and practice, you can achieve a realistic perspective on what's happening to you. When it hits you hard, take a moment to be mindful. Assess and name your emotions. Be objective. Allow them to exist and know that they're not good or bad. Your ability to experience the full spectrum of human emotion, even the unpleasant parts, is a beautiful thing.

With an objective view of what you're experiencing inside, firmly remind yourself that you deserve the thing you want, and you can have it. If you don't believe it yet, say it out loud. Repeat it until you feel some of your strength return, and then keep telling yourself every day, whether you feel it that day or not.

If there are details about the situation that continue to convince you that you're not enough, take some quiet time to assess those details objectively, the same way you looked at your feelings, and determine what factors you can control to overcome those details. It might be that you can have a healthy relationship, just not with this man, or you can have the career you want, but not in this company.

The way you respond in those moments will change the course of your life. This is where your strength is tested. Instead of wallowing in self-deprecation, look at the situation as a problem that can be solved, not a testament to your lack of value. What isn't working? Why isn't it working? What can you do to fix it?

You're not going to wake up some morning and discover that you're suddenly happy. You have to generate your happiness from inside. You must manipulate your world so that it can facilitate happiness. It starts with embracing who you are.

Your inherent worth lives in your potential to blossom, love, achieve, ignite, and change the world. Your worth is not dependent on anyone's willingness to see your potential and your value. You are enough, just as you are right now, and there is a lifetime of joy ahead of you.

Parting Thoughts

1. You are fearfully and wonderfully made. Celebrate your individuality and recognize the strength that lies within you.

2. Prioritize your well-being starting now. Nurture your mind, body, and soul. Take time for yourself. Indulge in activities that bring you joy and replenish your spirit.

3. We connect with others through vulnerability. Allow yourself to be open. Share your authentic self with those you trust.

4. Honest and open communication is the foundation of any healthy relationship. Listen with empathy and express your feelings with kindness and respect.

5. Lift each other up. Celebrate the dreams and accomplishments of the women in your life. Support and cheer for them, and they'll likely do the same for you.

6. Surround yourself with a tribe of supportive women who can see your journey, challenges, and victories. You can overcome any obstacle together.

7. Laughter is the best medicine. Look for humor and joy in everyday moments. Share laughter with your loved ones. It has the power to lighten the load on your shoulders.

Remember, my dear women and men, that you are not alone. We are all navigating the complexities of life. We all seek understanding and love.

As you strive to understand your partner, welcome love into your life, clarify your path, or create a healthier self-image, approach each day with an open heart. Lead with empathy and a willingness to grow. Celebrate the unique perspectives that everyone brings to the table.

May your journey be filled with joy, understanding, and deep connection.

CLOSING PRAYER

Gracious and Loving God,

As we near the end of this journey, we bow before you in gratitude and awe for the strength and inspiration you bestowed upon us to write and share the stories of women's struggles and love.

Thank you, Lord, for the courage and resilience that allowed us to capture the essence of these real-life experiences, delve into the depths of pain, emerge with hope, touch hearts, and stir souls with words of empowerment.

We are humbled, Father, by your presence, for it is in you that we find our truest strength. You have guided our words and filled them with grace. We acknowledge that your divine touch brings healing and transformation to those who read these words.

In scripture, we find wisdom and solace, words that transcend time and speak to our souls. As we close this book, we are reminded of Proverbs 31:25. "She is clothed with strength and dignity, and she laughs without fear of the future."

May the words within these pages and the power of your Word resonate deeply within the hearts of our readers. Let these stories of struggle ignite a flame of hope. May these tales of love inspire acts of compassion.

We pray, Father, that this book reaches the hands of those who need it most, those searching for solace, encouragement, and empowerment. May this be a catalyst for transformation, a tool that breaks chains and lifts spirits.

We surrender the impact of this book into your hands. May it find its way to hearts that long for healing and souls seeking strength and affirmation. May our readers plant these seeds here today and harvest growth tomorrow. May these women embrace their worth, rise above adversity, and walk in the radiant light of your love.

In the name of Jesus, our Savior and Redeemer, we offer up this prayer with our trust in your divine plan.

Amen